WRITERS

ON

WRITERS

Published in partnership with

STATE LIBRARY
VICTORIA
What's your story?

WRITERS
TONY
BIRCH
ON
KIM
SCOTT
WRITERS

Black Inc.

Published by Black Inc.
in association with the University of Melbourne and State Library Victoria.

Black Inc., an imprint of Schwartz Books Pty Ltd
Wurundjeri Country
22–24 Northumberland Street, Collingwood VIC 3066, Australia
enquiries@blackincbooks.com
www.blackincbooks.com

State Library Victoria
328 Swanston Street, Melbourne Victoria 3000 Australia
www.slv.vic.gov.au

The University of Melbourne
Parkville Victoria 3010 Australia
www.unimelb.edu.au

9781760644796 (hardback)
9781743823545 (ebook)

 A catalogue record for this
book is available from the
National Library of Australia

Cover design by Peter Long and Aira Pimping
Typesetting by Aira Pimping
Photograph of Kim Scott by Janine Sheen
Photograph of Tony Birch by Savanna Kruger

Printed in China by 1010 Printing.

I was first struck by the power of Kim Scott's writing while I was far from home, in both a physical and cultural sense. In 2003, I was in the US, staying at Harvard University, outside Boston. I'd been invited to speak at an Australian Studies conference. The gathering attracted major Australian writers and thinkers, including Gail Jones, Frank Moorhouse, David Malouf and Meaghan Morris. Our hosts were generous, accommodating us at the well-appointed Harvard Inn, where we enjoyed the hospitality of big beds, big bathtubs and, in the tradition of American culinary excess, big servings at every meal. Although I'm a non-drinker, I enjoyed the company at the nightly gatherings in the inn with other conference attendees. We shared stories and engaged in civil debate, while several of my Australian colleagues liberally sampled the many Australian wines on offer. By the evening of the last day of our visit, the cellar lay almost bare, with not a drop of Australian red or white to be found.

The warm reception by our hosts extended to a welcoming dinner on the opening night of the conference, held at the prestigious Harvard Club. A history of colonial conquest dominates the walls, in paintings, photographs and memorial plaques to great men and the occasional woman. The meal that night was sumptuous, and the hospitality was again warm, except for an uncomfortable moment at the commencement of the night when it appeared that I might not be allowed to enter the club at all, as I was not wearing a required tie. I was, though, sporting two collars: a white shirt collar and another that graced my distinctly 'Melbourne black' woollen cardigan. Fine merino, in fact. I'd been waiting to enter the club alongside another Australian academic, who had, in preparation for the night ahead, fuelled himself with several glasses of red back at the inn. He was wearing a shabby flannel shirt, a borrowed jacket several sizes too small for him and a tie that could have been mistaken for a soiled handkerchief. Yet he had no trouble at all getting into the club, as his outfit matched the dress code, at least in a technical sense. Perhaps the woman guarding the door thought he was in period costume, playing a character out of *Dad and Dave*? After accepting a lurid floral tie, I was also welcomed into the club.

The paper I presented the following day, 'The First White Man Born', was concerned with the history of the Stolen Generations in Australia; being the theft of Aboriginal and Torres Strait Islander children from their families and communities through the twentieth century. My paper also interrogated populist right-wing responses to the Human Rights and Equal Opportunity Commission's *Bringing Them Home* report, which had been released in 1997. The report followed hearings across Australia that gathered evidence from hundreds of survivors of child removal. Victims told of the violence inflicted on them in government-run institutions and religious orphanages and as foster children in private homes. The evidence presented was so harrowing that some conversations could only be heard and recorded 'in camera'.

The Harvard gathering was well attended, and attracted Australians living and working in the US, as well as representatives of the Australian government, including several consular officials. The prime minister at the time was John Howard. During my presentation, I made comments that were critical of specific remarks he'd made in response to the release of *Bringing*

Them Home. As I spoke, several audience members shifted awkwardly in their seats, in particular a group of men in suits in the front row. Kim Scott's 1999 novel, *Benang: From the Heart*, was a key text informing my presentation. Towards the end of the talk, I quoted words that are forced upon *Benang*'s violent white patriarch, Ern Scat, by his 'mixed-blood' grandson, Harley. 'Ern Solomon Scat', I announced to the auditorium, channelling the words of both Harley and the author, 'fucks chooks … fucked all his family before him.'

The poetic statement was not well received by some in the audience. 'Fucks chooks?' one man whispered to another, a bewildered look on his face. 'Did he say "Fucks chooks?"', he repeated. 'Chooks?' My comments caused some discomfort. The criticism that followed focused not on this quote from *Benang*, nor on concern for any chook that may have been harmed during an act of white male bestiality, but on my perceived disrespect for Australia expressed while on the other side of the globe.

Nationalism cannot escape its parochialism, particularly when being articulated 'offshore'. I had not fully grasped the fact that I was attending a gathering that, to a great degree, was intended to be a 'celebration of the nation'. Others in the room, several academics and representatives of the Australian government, let me know that Harvard was not the place to discuss what was described to me as the 'internal politics' of Australia. However, the writing of Kim Scott was the very antithesis of a shallow flag-waving exercise. The reception of my discussion of his use of fiction to interrogate both historical and contemporary politics in Australia revealed not so much the sensitivities of some audience members (although those were clearly apparent) but that Scott was just the writer we needed during a period of cultural upheaval in Australia.

My second meeting with Kim Scott was more personal. It took place literally at the centre of Australia, in the Sails in the Desert hotel near Uluru. I'd been invited to a five-day screenwriting workshop, organised by the Indigenous unit of Screen Australia. The workshop was led by the renowned filmmaker Rachel Perkins and the screenwriter and director Guillermo Arriaga, the author of scripts for major films including *Amores Perros* (2000), *21 Grams* (2003), *The Three Burials of Melquiades Estrada* (2005) and *Babel* (2006). Other writers invited to the workshop included Dylan Coleman, Bruce Pascoe, Melissa Lucashenko, Dub Leffler – and Scott.

My first impression of Kim in person was that he was warm and friendly, and just a little bit cheeky in a generous way, which didn't surprise me at all. He is a person with a quick sense of humour, delivered with laconic ease. Both Scott's physical stature and his mannerisms reminded me of one of my favourite screen actors, Jack Lemmon, in particular the deadpan, and occasionally tragic, face he wears in films such as *The Apartment* (1960) – a look that Lemmon was always able to shift to a childlike grin in an instant. I didn't realise at the time the extent to which Kim Scott's personality and demeanour reflect characters in both *Benang* and his following novel, *That Deadman Dance* (2010). These are Noongar men who somehow manage to balance profound sadness and trauma with a degree of humour that deceptively undermines colonial attempts to subjugate the Aboriginal body.

Harley, the protagonist of *Benang*, is a playful character. A sly wink here and there is used to disarm readers, before he grabs their attention with stories of the utmost power. Likewise, in *That Deadman Dance*, Bobby Wabalanginy, a Noongar man, travels across time, space and place, providing a lens on the past for readers. Bobby is a street performer and discarded fringe-dweller, entertaining Settlers who have seemingly won control over his Country. In some scenes in the novel, Bobby appears as an endearing child, an *innocent*, witness to and documentarian of the colonial violence that increasingly damages both the culture and the natural ecologies of Noongar people. He becomes a repository of memories, of stories of loss, dislocation and colonial neglect.

As with the characters in his novels, Scott himself inhabits a range of guises, faces he wears to interrogate the complex and messy frontier history of colonial encounters. He is a writer, storyteller and researcher, a conduit working within the Noongar community to recover and retell stories from an Aboriginal perspective, be it a narrative examining 'first contacts' with the British on Noongar territory in the early nineteenth century, a creative interrogation of a book published by a racist 'protector' over a century later or a story of violence that takes place in a prison cell in the twenty-first century. Kim Scott's literary voice is a choir, and we are fortunate to have been offered his song.

My own academic training was in history. I completed my PhD at Melbourne University in 2003 and taught Australian and Aboriginal History for several years. I was also, for a short period, involved in the History Wars of the late 1990s and early 2000s, an undignified exercise whereby politically motivated populists – intellectuals and politicians both – picked over a carcass of footnotes in yet another attempt to delegitimise the rights and authority of Aboriginal and Torres Strait Islander people. I became disheartened by the behaviour of the history profession, once described to me by a colleague as the 'self-appointed aristocracy of the humanities', around the time that I began to think more seriously about other forms of storytelling that might inform us about the past. I became interested in film, still photography, writing and oral storytelling.

I was attracted to Kim Scott's writing not only for its rich approach to storytelling but also for the way he understood the power of the colonial archive. Rather than regard it as a set of neutral and objective facts, Scott knew that paper, ink and the written word produced highly selective and subjective stories of Australia's colonial past. He also realised that if he were to extract a counter-narrative from the archive, to force it to confess to truths camouflaged by bureaucratic language, he could use fiction to great effect.

I value Kim Scott's fiction because it prods me to consider the lives of Noongar people and the courage they have shown when faced with the onslaught of invader violence. Through a discussion of his novels, I want to explore fiction as a pathway to truth. I have no interest in arguing over the relative truth of fiction and history writing (I'll let some other dog chase that tail), or the power of a metaphor versus the footnote. I do not regard fiction to be in a contest with the discipline of history. Fiction is more than able to validate truth without having to defer to capital-H history. With all the talk of 'truth-telling' in Australia, some of it worthwhile and some clichéd, Kim Scott's writing provides an invaluable entry point to a meaningful dialogue.

BENANG: FROM THE HEART

In 2000, Kim Scott was announced as the joint winner of the Miles Franklin Literary Award for his second novel, *Benang: From the Heart,* alongside Thea Astley, for her book *Drylands*, both published in 1999. Scott, the first Aboriginal writer to be presented with the award, would win a second time, in 2011, for *That Deadman Dance.* In addition to the bookends of Miles Franklins, Scott's fiction has been widely recognised through other awards, including the Commonwealth Writers' Prize in 2011, also for *That Deadman Dance*, and several premier's literary prizes.

Scott is also published widely as a non-fiction writer, and with the Noongar Elder Hazel Brown, his auntie, he wrote the ground-breaking *Kayang and Me* (2005), which was the culmination of extensive research by the co-authors, utilising oral storytelling and Noongar language systems, in collaboration with other members of the Noongar community. The goal of *Kayang and Me* was to preserve and share stories of Noongar history and culture and promote their relevance to contemporary society. Scott also has a key role in the Wirlomin Noongar Language and Stories Project (www.wirlomin.com.au), which strives to empower members of his community by sharing stories and history, both within their own Mob and with the wider community.

Whichever genre Scott works in, Noongar language is at the heart of his writing, as is a critical engagement with written and spoken English, a language that was customarily used to subjugate and stifle the voices of Aboriginal people. While Aboriginal storytelling has often been relegated to the status of 'folklore' and 'myth' in Western literary traditions, Scott addresses not only orality as central in reviving Aboriginal culture and languages but also, importantly, storytelling as an intellectual and creative tool. In the 2020s, with 'truth-telling' becoming both a demand from Aboriginal people and, perhaps unfortunately, a populist buzzword, Kim Scott uses storytelling to address truths of the past that some would prefer we left silent and undocumented.

While Scott is known in the literary world as a *writer,* an *individual*, his role as an Aboriginal storyteller is more complex and inclusive. The characters and voices on the pages of Scott's fiction are clearly the product of his fertile imagination and powerful intellect. He is an author equipped with a sharp eye, wit, an ethical ear and a big heart. His storytelling technique is dignified and democratic. He accepts a cultural responsibility that Aboriginal writers generally welcome. Scott's work is communal in that his writing also draws on the stories of generations of Aboriginal people who came before him; people who had their own voices and stories stolen from them. It is unsurprising to know that Scott regards his writing and story-gathering as driven by a passionate commitment 'to restor[e] a positive sense of community to a historically oppressed and dispossessed people'.[1]

The commitment that he speaks of is evident in *Benang*. The novel deals with the experiences of Noongar people subject to iterations of the *Aborigines Act* in Western Australia during the first half of the twentieth century, and the impact and trauma visited on subsequent generations. The novel also draws attention to white Australia's obsession with Aboriginal identities and the ludicrous but at times tragic outcome of identity legislation, driven by a fixation with skin colour and the 'taint of dark blood'.[2]

This is a story of the state violence that underpinned the 'uplifting' of Aboriginal people. The history is articulated through the novel's narrator, Harley, an Aboriginal man whose life has been determined by caste, his 'mixed blood'. He has been raised by his white grandfather, Ernest Solomon Scat, a man who prizes his grandson as not only 'the brightest and most useful in the uplifted state' but also, potentially, *the first* [true] *white man born* as a result of quasi-eugenicist and forced separation policies that, if successful, would have meant the eventual extinction of 'full-blooded' Aboriginal people.

The non-Aboriginal characters in *Benang*, including Ern Scat, are both witnesses to, and perpetrators of, colonial violence. Not surprisingly, the Settler characters in *Benang* are hesitant to speak openly of aspects of their behaviour towards Aboriginal people, in particular the sexual violence that accompanies the outwardly benign language of the state bureaucracy supporting their authoritarian intervention into Aboriginal daily life. It's perhaps an odd and interesting idea that an author can demand that their characters speak of something they would prefer not to address. Scott demands that these men do speak of their past acts of violence, even though they do so unwillingly. They are also spoken about, exposed, through Harley and his Aboriginal uncles Jack and Will, the great storytellers of *Benang*.

Kim Scott suffers from what we in the research community self-diagnose as the affliction of 'archive fever'. He has spent endless hours on a textual archaeological dig, an investigation involving index cards, dust-covered government reports, esoteric notes sent between government officials and photographs of unnamed and lost family members. Through his research, Scott has not only uncovered and reconstructed a history of Aboriginal lives subject to the colonial bureaucracy. He has also assiduously exposed the architects of racially motivated policies and legislation that amount to attempted genocide.

Scott has commented that although working with colonial archival records left him feeling troubled, the knowledge he gained, assisted by the 'perverse energy' he experienced reading the colonial narrative, was channelled into the writing of *Benang*. While it might be too strong a comment to suggest that this energy equipped him with an urge to creative revenge, the novel certainly speaks back to the empire, through the Aboriginal characters who refuse subservience and speak *out of turn* with grace and courage.

Whether on Country with other Noongar people or working within the walls of government records offices, Kim Scott demands that the colonial archive does speak with a more transparent voice, exposing its true political and psychological intentions. As Harley's forebears – women – were tied to the bedposts of white Settler men and abused, Scott's creation, Harley, in turn pins down the archive and extracts a confession from it. He is also determined that the stories told by his family members resonate into the present, that the experiences of people are transferred from one generation to the next.

Scott, along with the Elders who have guided him and trust him as a storyteller, is a custodian of language, from a single vocal sound accompanied by the beat of a hand on heart to *big* stories, narratives of places and people forever evolving, stories continually expanding that will never again be harnessed and controlled by non-Aboriginal people. These are stories that can never be fully expressed, such is their richness. Like healthy Country, healthy stories, even those that make some feel less than 'relaxed and comfortable' (John Howard's preferred version of history-telling), are nurtured by 'the revival and regeneration of an ancestral language'.

Despite the collective grief experienced by the Aboriginal characters in *Benang*, and the wanton cruelty inflicted by 'protectors', other government officials and police, Scott's fictional witness and scribe, Harley, often expresses himself with a sly wink towards his readers, turning to humour – as a weapon – that is so sharp and so quick that, yes, if you blink you might just miss it. Scott has great respect for the past, the deep-time history he shares with other Noongar people. I suspect that he also regards aspects of colonial history, such as first contacts between Aboriginal people and the British, as at times surreal, as is expressed occasionally in the tone of *That Deadman Dance*. And as much as attempts to 'breed out' the identity of Aboriginal people in the twentieth century were driven by state-sanctioned cruelty, resulting in harm and intergenerational trauma, in *Benang* we witness scenes of colonial absurdity that, in other circumstances, would not be out of place in a Monty Python skit.

WE ARE STILL HERE

The colonial version of Australian history is dependent on a set of mythologies. One of the many problems embedded in white Australia's understanding of itself is that national hubris and confidence rely on fictions that are presented as an unproblematic set of facts, commencing with the notion of *terra nullius* itself: an empty land awaiting British civilisation and occupation. During my training as a historian, it became clear to me that while the discipline preached objectivity, as with any other form of narrative production, researching and writing history is an emotionally charged and subjective practice. The problem for historians, as I saw it then, is that practitioners feared being open about their own position, particularly on political grounds.

Regarding colonial history and the violence and attempted dispossession of Aboriginal and Torres Strait Islander people, there is much at stake, even for those on the supposed 'good side' of the discipline, the left-of-centre liberal historians. This was clear in Australia during the History Wars debates, when serious tensions arose between historians seemingly defending Indigenous people from attacks by populist conservatives, and Indigenous people, who felt that our white 'friends' on the left had brought an *objective* gun to a *political* knife fight.

Fiction, of course, also produces stories of national unity, whitewashing and occasional flag-waving. I value Kim Scott's fiction so highly because I feel that his approach to fiction is to put the flags aside. *That Deadman Dance* asks us not to consider who we were so much as who we could be, collectively, in the future. Scott understands that stories of the past cannot be projected in a neat, linear manner if they are to be told ethically and honestly. The past is a bumpy road, littered with potholes and obstacles. Therefore, attempting to summarise the plot and structure of *Benang* is no straightforward task. The novel is not plot-driven in the traditional sense. It contains several beginnings and middles, but has no ending as such. When I first read *Benang*, I was desperate for plot and a climactic ending, eager that the violence of Settler men, government administrators and citizens alike would be exposed, and that the perpetrators of crimes against Aboriginal people would be punished. Regardless of my desire for simple wish fulfilment, the novel plots a more complex, and more truthful, path. Those who committed acts of violence against Indigenous people were rarely punished. While the villains of history may meet a bloody end in a Tarantino film, Scott has no interest in pure escapism.

The literary scholar Ruby Lowe writes that Kim Scott 'makes explicit the sexual motivations of the infamous West Australian administrator A.O. Neville, and illuminates the ways in which his eugenicist government policies were reliant on the sexual desires and practices of Settlers'; men who camouflage violence with a language of colonial benevolence and quasi-science.[3] These men are the villains of the story, and as a reader I wanted justice for the Noongar characters.

In a conventional novel, the narrative might have climaxed in a scene of retribution. But true to the history that informs the novel, *Benang* provides no such outcome for Noongar people. Instead, their survival itself, after having been confronted by the onslaught of invasion, in all its guises, becomes a quiet moment of triumph.

The last line of the novel is 'We are still here, Benang'. *Still here.* A direct and profound statement loaded with cultural meaning and political history for Aboriginal people having confronted the myths of *terra nullius*. 'Still here' reminds us that the story continues, moving forward, reaching back, and circling itself. Always.

Nurturing the story of *Benang* in his hands, the 'edgy and awkward' Harley is both an unreliable narrator and a truth-seeker. He evades certainty, and refuses a simplistic narrative of colonial superiority, while he embarks on a journey to recover the stories of the Aboriginal family and community he is descended from. While some literary critics have depicted Harley as something of a lost character, 'a blank sheet' who 'does not know who he is', I believe that he is always in control of the complex, non-linear story he weaves.[4]

Harley is a trickster, in the Aboriginal tradition. He plays with his reader, albeit in a respectful manner, much as he does with the story itself. The advice of another Miles Franklin award-winner, Alexis Wright (for her 2013 novel, *Carpentaria*), might be helpful when reading *Benang*. Reflecting on the comment that her own novels may prove too 'difficult' for some readers, Wright responded that she writes not for the 'tourist reader' but for those who accept that while fiction may provide comfort for some readers, it is necessary work for others.[5] Readers of *Benang* are expected to bring effort to the text, to work, as also noted by Lowe: 'Reading *Benang* is not like following a singular narrative or even a narrative with sub-plots,' she writes, 'it more closely approximates interpreting a complex set of registers and interwoven realities.'

The Noongar characters in *Benang* live under constant surveillance. When not physically shackled by the state, people are forced to remain on the move, evading legislative controls, diligently modifying their behaviour to avoid the panoptical gaze of colonial authorities. Families become separated, some by force, others by way of occasional denial of blood, kin and cultural links, in the effort to remain outside the framework of the 'act', the policies that corralled Aboriginal people by using ever-shifting identity categories that not only denied people the right to self-determination but also disorientated and disabled them.

The emotional toll of the Protection Acts on the Noongar community in *Benang* is horrendous. People are subject to incarceration, beatings, murder and, in the case of women and girls, endemic sexual violence resulting in the birth of 'mixed-blood' children, who themselves subsequently suffer lives of abuse. Those few who manage to free themselves from the clutches of the state experience lives of cultural isolation; having 'passed' to survive, they undergo self-abandonment, as expressed by Uncle Will when he states, 'I have tried to keep away from Aboriginals ... it has made me very lonely, all my life.'

Initially *Benang* appears to be a literary jigsaw puzzle. Imagine the pieces of the novel as self-contained scenes, laid out before you on a table. Some pieces easily connect to each other. Others do not. Do not try to force the pieces together, as they will refuse your efforts. It is important, when challenged with such a narrative puzzle, that the reader keep faith with the artist who created it. A reader of *Benang* 'has to piece the story together and reconstruct it, just as Harley had to',[6] the reward for effort being that the pieces gradually do come together and compose a revelatory narrative – no piece of the puzzle is left without its place in the story, or within the external history informing the novel.

What we realise at the conclusion of *Benang* is that Harley is not 'hovering' at all. He is grounded on Country. His identity is not fragmented, and he cannot fulfil his grandfather's perverse fantasy and become *the first white man born*. He is a Noongar man, brought to life by the stories of his uncles and the courage of his community. The novel reflects the journey of many Indigenous people separated from family, disenfranchised from Country. Their lives do become fractured, and piecing themselves together requires bravery and effort. As readers, we are able to share in this effort and be rewarded.

While refusing a standard literary structure, be it plot or linearity, *Benang* is ultimately a work of coherence. It may be helpful to imagine Kim

Scott as a literary bowerbird, curiously gathering scraps of paper, snippets of whispered conversations, truth and lies both, muted by *the great Australian silence*, a state of mind more than a place, which has historically refused to *listen* to writing and storytelling that interrogates Australia's colonial past. *Benang* is a generous offering from a writer seeking to shift not only our conversations but also our collective understanding of who we are as a nation, both Aboriginal and non-Aboriginal. Kim Scott is a gentle combatant fighting injustice. And he is on our side – each of ours. Scott uses words, sentences, images and stories to confront racism, a blight that for him 'burns like a pox and a plague and is incubated at the centre of how we live and organise ourselves'.[7]

BRINGING THEM HOME

*B*enang was written during a period of tremendous racial and political upheaval in Australia, with tensions surrounding conflicting versions of colonial history, the ongoing issue of land rights, and shocking evidence of the historical abuse of the human rights of Aboriginal and Torres Strait Islander people across the twentieth century that would culminate in the eruption of the History Wars in the late 1990s. The national pressures centred on race relations between Aboriginal and non-Aboriginal people had been building for more than a decade. In 1987, the Commonwealth government established the Royal Commission into Aboriginal Deaths in Custody to investigate the many hundreds of Aboriginal people who had died in prisons, cells and, on occasion, in their own homes when facing arrest. The findings of the commission would reverberate through the 1990s, due to the dissatisfaction of Aboriginal organisations and community groups who would lead campaigns over the refusal of Commonwealth and state authorities to implement any of the 333 recommendations of the royal commission.

While Scott was writing *Benang*, the *Bringing Them Home* report was released to the public. The document destroyed any notion that governments, federal and state, had acted with benevolence towards Aboriginal children who had been removed from their families. The collective narrative of Aboriginal adults recalling the traumas they suffered as removed children shook the foundations of existing histories that supported an unproblematic national narrative of settlement and assimilation. The backlash from conservatives would yet again devastate the lives of Aboriginal people who had recalled their harrowing childhood experiences in good faith, in the hope of receiving justice. The report was subject to intense political and media scrutiny, with populist commentators going so far as to assert that there was no Stolen Generation in Australia, let alone *generations* of sufferers. Furthermore, some made the shocking claim that Aboriginal people who had been institutionalised as children had subsequently suffered from false memory syndrome when giving evidence to the enquiry.

John Howard had been elected prime minister a year earlier, in 1996. He is famously remembered for railing against the 'black armband' view of white Australia's past and had no time for the revisionist histories documented in the *Bringing Them Home* report. He'd also vigorously opposed the views expressed by the immediate past prime minister, Paul Keating, in his Redfern speech of 1992. Howard's response to the stories of Stolen Generations members reported during the enquiry was defensive and objectionable, as far as Aboriginal people were concerned. Introducing his Sir Thomas Playford Memorial Lecture in July 1996, Howard's position on any critique of colonial history was clearly stated. The prime minister objected to ordinary Australians being 'force-fed by those self-appointed cultural dietitians in our midst whose agenda has more to do with divisive political strategies than respect for the facts of history'. Later that year, in an extensive interview with the popular *Who Weekly* magazine, Howard elaborated: 'Although we did treat Aborigines appallingly, I'm not one of those who say that whenever there is criticism made of Australia or Australian history we should roll over in a grovelling apology to the rest of the world.'

The Howard government would subsequently make no apology to the Stolen Generations, grovelling or otherwise. Outside the confines of formal politics and a populist-driven history war, it was becoming more widely accepted, as a result of the detailed testimonies in *Bringing Them Home*, that change was needed. Those who had suffered abuse were owed a debt by the nation in the form of a public apology (as recommended in the report). Subsequently, in 2000, the same year that *Benang* was awarded the Miles Franklin, hundreds of thousands of people, mostly non-Aboriginal, marched in cities and towns across Australia in support of reconciliation and recompense for the Stolen Generations. A formal apology was finally delivered in the Commonwealth parliament by Labor prime minister Kevin Rudd in 2007.

In his Redfern speech, Paul Keating had challenged white Australians to consider a situation in which their own lives were systematically violated. 'Imagine if our spiritual life was denied and ridiculed', he asked, and 'imagine if we had suffered the injustice and then were blamed for it'. In 2000, two Aboriginal people, Lorna Cubillo and Peter Gunner, both taken from their families as children, would ask the Commonwealth to imagine such crimes and provide compensation for the suffering they had endured as kids. In his summary judgement at the conclusion of the federal court case, Justice Maurice O'Loughlin described the appalling conditions that both children had been subjected to:

> I accepted Mrs Cubillo's evidence that she was viciously assaulted by a missionary on the staff of the home and I accepted her evidence that she was very unhappy and starved for affection during her time at

Retta Dixon [Home] ... I accepted Mr Gunner's evidence that he had a most unhappy childhood at St Mary's and I accept that he was the victim of a sexual assault by one of the missionaries during his time at St Mary's.[8]

Regardless of his own conclusions, Justice O'Loughlin found that the Commonwealth had no case to answer, as, under Article 6 of the Northern Territory's Aboriginal Ordinance, 'the Director of Native Affairs was permitted to take Aboriginal children into custody if he believed this to be in the best interest of the child'. Those interests were obviously not met. The story of Lorna Cubillo and Peter Gunner is heartbreaking, and the judgement was truly shocking. While O'Loughlin stated repeatedly that he was *convinced* of their suffering, Cubillo and Gunner received no justice at all. When Kim Scott states that the craft of fiction allows him 'to rethink and possibly to retrieve or create something from between and behind the lines of the page', it is not only the pages of colonial archives he is referring to.[9] Scott's fiction also exposes the perversity of colonial justice in Australia.

'DILUTE THE STRAIN'

While Kim Scott is a dedicated researcher, his literary creation Harley is suspicious of government paper, even when it helps him piece together an insight into his own past and that of the Noongar community. 'Hovering over documents, filed in plastic envelopes in rumbling drawers and snapping files', Harley is repeatedly confronted by evidence of the attempted destruction of Aboriginal life. His white grandfather, Ern, as was the case with the real-life Chief Protector of Aboriginal people, A.O. Neville, relies on fractions, equations and mathematics to create the 'certain' but crude categories of *full-blood*, *half-caste (first cross)*, *quadroon*, *octoroon*. The labels are then used to restrict Aboriginal freedom of movement, specifically through control of bodies, denying the reproductive autonomy of Aboriginal women in order to 'dilute the strain' of Aboriginal blood over time, a self-consciously deceptive euphemism for genocide.

Harley interrogates government documents, Ern's years of 'research'. He then undermines the authority of the archive by contrasting it with the stories told by his uncles, producing a powerful counter-narrative. Rifling through Ern's papers, Harley informs us that he 'shuffled idly through them. I was careless, letting them fall to the floor.' He does so partly to highlight his disregard for the sanitised colonial narrative, and also to torment his grandfather, who is reliant on the story of the archive for his own legitimacy, a record of paternalistic 'uplifting' that has no interest in documenting the story of the sexual and physical abuse of Aboriginal people.

Ern's paper record can only offer Harley lies. To validate his own story, one that will connect him with Noongar people, he requires the support of Uncle Jack and Uncle Will. The juxtaposition of the Aboriginal oral narrative with colonial documents puts the written archive on trial. As 'judge, jury and executioner', Harley punishes its custodian, his grandfather, who has become physically immobilised with age and depends on his grandson for his care. Their roles in life have been reversed. It is the young man who now controls the body of his former master. Having taken charge of Ern's 'carefully and meticulously filed documents', Harley seeks revenge for the abuse he has suffered. Driven by a desire to undermine the paper story Ern had gathered, Harley torments the old man by burning his meticulous records: 'One at a time I held each before his eyes, put a match to it, and let it fall when the flame reached my fingers.'

Harley also forces his grandfather to become a repository of the stories of violence recalled by his uncles. More disturbingly (perhaps), the old man's body itself becomes a document, a sheet of paper, in a sense, recording a history of the abuse of others. When the uncles retell a story of past violence, both physical and sexual, committed against Aboriginal women and children, Harley takes pleasure in the knowledge that his grand-father cannot avoid absorbing the conversation. Once he is forced to hear these stories, they cannot be simply erased. When the stories are told around a campfire by the uncles, Harley remarks that 'old Ern, almost immobile, has closed his eyes. No doubt he wished he could close his ears also.'

While it is in Ern Scat's interest to forget his past interactions with Aboriginal women,

Harley, in a 'shrill voice, like the mind', confronts his grandfather's selective amnesia with stories that expose his lies. Harley goes further, tying his grandfather to a chair, as white men once tied Aboriginal women to bedposts, and carves the words 'END, CRASH, FINISH' – a horror story – into his grandfather's skin, rendering the white male body a monument to its own evil. As cruel as his actions may appear, Harley's scarring of his grandfather's skin is a visceral reminder that words, language itself, can at times be as violent as physical acts.

AUSTRALIA'S COLOURED MINORITY

The acknowledgements pages of *Benang* list key government sources referred to by Scott, including royal commission evidence from government officials agonising over the refusal of Aboriginal communities to simply 'die out', as had been predicted during the decades of the late nineteenth and early twentieth centuries. A.O. Neville's *Australia's Coloured Minority: Its Place in the Community* is a key text for *Benang*, one from which Scott drew inspiration and, I suspect, some urgency. It is through Neville's faith in eugenics, blood quantum theorisation and the resulting 'breeding out' of race that Scott's creation, Ern Scat, was able to rationalise his cruelty.

It is a common belief among historians, social scientists and legal scholars that Aboriginal women and girls experienced sexual and physical violence at the hands of Settler men because of policies and practices, including incarceration in its various manifestations, that rendered victims vulnerable, and ultimately silenced them. In other words, Settler men took advantage of an existing disempowerment and deprivation to fulfil their sexual desires. *Benang* presents us with an inversion of this argument, producing an even more disturbing conclusion. It is a story of calculation and orchestration, whereby Settler men appointed to protect Aboriginal women and children established a state-sanctioned system that would allow abuse that had previously occurred on the 'frontier' to continue unimpeded, within the civilised world of the institution and a supportive bureaucratic framework.

Ern Scat is obsessed with A.O. Neville's system of genealogical charts, photographs and evidentiary captions, such as 'FIRST CROSS Half-blood mother with her quadroon child' and '3. Octaroon Grandson – Father Australian of Irish descent; Mother No. 2'.[10] Neville becomes Scat's mentor and absent collaborator, which should come as no surprise. In life, the chief protector of Aborigines in Western Australia was at one time a mentor to the nation in matters regarding white Australia's ubiquitous 'Aboriginal Problem'.

A.O. Neville dominated legislation controlling the lives and wellbeing of Aboriginal people in Western Australia for several decades in the first half of the twentieth century. He was widely regarded as a national expert on 'native affairs' until his retirement in 1940. In 1937, the Commonwealth government organised the first (and only) centralised conference dealing with 'Aboriginal welfare' in Australia. Representatives from each state were invited to Canberra, except for members of the Tasmanian government, which claimed to have rid itself of any 'Aboriginal problem'.

The aim of the Canberra gathering was to 'ultimately absorb ... natives of aboriginal origin, but not of full blood' into the wider community, and to 'preserve as far as possible the uncivilized native in his normal tribal estate'. Neville, an invited guest at the two-day event, outlined the 'successes of legislative controls in Western Australia', including his crude blood quantum experiments. It was widely accepted that his views would influence whatever policies other states might adopt to comply with the Commonwealth's ultimate desire, being the eventual 'uniformity of legislation' across the country.[11]

(It is worth noting that conference delegates were aware that the deprivations suffered by Aboriginal people living 'under the act' could result in conflict and protest, as had already occurred in several states. The response of the conference to potential unrest was 'to obtain full information upon racial problems in America and South Africa for submission to a further conference of Chief Protectors'.)

Neville is regarded as the father of caste legislation in Australia. He certainly is in *Benang*, where his spectre shadows the narrative. But he was not the first legislator to use categories of identity and ideas of blood quantum to control Aboriginal people. To begin to understand a national history of caste legislation in this country, it is necessary to examine (albeit briefly) what occurred in the colony of Victoria during the mid-to-late nineteenth century. Victoria's

Aborigines Act would become the national template following the federation of the British colonies in 1901.

It was only after 1851, when Victoria became a colony independent of New South Wales, that white Settlers turned to ideas of 'civilising the blacks through a legislative framework supported by systems of incarceration. In 1886, the Victorian parliament legislated an *Aborigines Act* that separated Aboriginal people according to caste and blood. While much of the language of the legislation was convoluted and inconsistent (as is so often the case, providing little or no certainty for Aboriginal people), its key objective was to remove all Aboriginal males under the age of thirty-five who were not 'of full blood' from government reserves and religious missions, while confining 'full-blooded' Aboriginal people, and all Aboriginal women, 'mixed-blood' or otherwise – by force, if necessary – on the same reserves and missions.

While 'mixed-blood' Aboriginal people would eventually be legislated out of existence, becoming if not white, at least a version of A.O. Neville's twentieth-century 'coloured minority', the more immediate objective of the legislation – to deal with the fate of 'full-blooded' Aboriginal people – was made clear: 'The Board has made a fair beginning of a policy which is the beginning of the end, and which, in the course of a few years, will leave only a few pure blacks under the care of Government.'[12]

That is, the eventual extinction of 'full-blooded' Aboriginal people was both envisaged and sought after. The term 'passed away', again masking the violence of intent, was incorporated in the Western Australian *Aborigines Act* of 1905, which inherited both the philosophy and human rights abuses of the Victorian legislation. In Kim Scott's attempt to 'read through and between the lines' of the archive, *Benang* confronts the staged banality of bureaucratic language and, equally damaging, the language of a taxonomic system, more suitable to the classification of animal species, that was created to legally separate and degrade Aboriginal people.

Ern Scat is a deranged doppelgänger created by Scott to expose the prejudices of A.O. Neville, a man who revelled in the belief that white blood was always superior, more resilient than that of the 'native'. It is reasonable to suggest that just as Harley eventually has total control of his grandfather, rendering him mute and impotent, one of Kim Scott's own desires is to symbolically castrate Neville. On his retirement, Neville dedicated himself to documenting his decades of experience with Aboriginal people, which resulted in the publication of his *Australia's Coloured Minority*.

The book is disturbing reading. Although Neville would never have intended it to be received as such, *Australia's Coloured Minority* is also a deeply sad book. The descriptive passages about Aboriginal life and the faces of people being photographed rely on a narrative of 'type' and 'specimen' for legitimation, rather than a story of people entitled to dignity and the expression of their own thoughts and emotions. Kim Scott is acutely aware of the abuse of social 'science' to dehumanise people who would then be treated with wanton disregard.

Although initially labelled a 'half-caste', an Aboriginal woman examined by Neville is celebrated in *Australia's Coloured Minority* as being 'unusually fair [with] very fine features. Very well spoken.'[13] Neville wants to share her potential with us. With his guidance, and total control of her life, it might just be possible for Neville to 'uplift' such women into white society. His claims about the success of assimilation are contrasted with a narrative of perceived neglect, even savagery. Images of children, framed by instructive captions such as 'As I found them' and 'A Bush Waif', are contrasted with an angelic but tragic portrait of an Aboriginal child after having been removed from Country and saved by his new 'Father'; 'Quadroon Boy – Child of Quadroon Parents.'

Uplifting Aboriginal people is presented as uninhibited progress, whereas the world in which Aboriginal people of mixed descent lived before being subjected to measures of control, including incarceration, remains primitive, and an ongoing threat to white society that must be policed. Deeply offensive terms, including 'Boong', 'Coon',

'Nigger', are hurled at Aboriginal people not only to 'inflict pain' but also to legitimate whatever forms of intervention suit the government of the day. The 'primitive' had to be subjugated, eliminated, for uplifting to occur, and derogatory language was a vital tool in producing such an outcome. According to Harley, 'Once you shared this tongue, you could taste it. Evolution. Light out of darkness.'

'ERN SOLOMON SCAT: HAS FAILED'

There are scenes in *Benang*, terrifying moments of darkness, that evoke comparisons with the contemporary abuse of Aboriginal children and youth in Australia. In addition to girls being targeted with sexual violence, young boys in *Benang*, existing on the margin of colonial occupation, are treated as nothing more than refuse, bodies to be punished and disposed of. For instance, an Aboriginal boy who has 'disobeyed' his white masters is 'pushed into a large hessian bag and hung' from a tree. Early in the novel, the body 'of a child. A boy,' is dumped on the edge of a regional town. Concern is not for the circumstances surrounding his death but for the threat his body poses, rendered 'a hazard to the town's health'. This disregard for Aboriginal children is reminiscent of similar acts of violence and neglect a century later in Australia, whereby Aboriginal children are portrayed as a constant menace to white society and, therefore, suffer horrific conditions within the criminal justice system.

The realities of disadvantage and racial injustice reinforced in *Benang* are that, inevitably, 'the white skin always wins'. The impurities of primitive blood and skin colour are at times couched in ecological language. The irony is brutal, considering that early European agricultural systems, and subsequently mining exploration, caused irreparable damage to Aboriginal Country. Settlers become fixated with the 'taint', the pollution of blood resulting from miscegenation. Racial purity, a white fantasy, is pursued in *Benang* through a belief in the need to dilute

Aboriginal blood, which the coloniser expects will only be obliterated when enough Aboriginal bodies have been contained, pacified and, if necessary, destroyed. The ultimate desire being that 'a small dirty stream' will eventually be transformed 'into a large and clear one'.

Ern Scat represents the pathological thinking of many white men. Rather than being motivated by an interest in assimilating Aboriginal people, to 'breed us out, fill us with shame', according to Harley, Ern's primary motivation is to fulfil his sexual appetite – 'all that rationalising to disguise his own desires', as Harley puts it. Ern visits an Aboriginal encampment in search of sexual gratification when he first arrives on the frontier. He is later reminded of what occurred there when asked, 'Have you seen the camps?' and remembers 'the first night [when] she turned her head away and her body took his thrusts'.

Later in the novel, when Ern has tired of his first Aboriginal wife, Kathleen, he turns his attentions to 'the girl Topsy ... extra fair skinned half-caste, perhaps ten years of age'. She is described as 'small and fine-boned as a bird ... almost a new species'. If Ern Scat is ever to celebrate the birth of 'the first white man born', it will be through violence, not love, science or benevolence. Topsy experiences this violence in an early encounter with Ern when he sexually assaults her in his bedroom before deciding that she will become his new wife. In old age, with Ern reduced to a state of impotence, in both a physical and a psychological sense, and helpless to avoid his grandson's torment, he suffers further humiliation. Harley, in an act he admits is neither 'noble or dignified', places a pen in Ern's hand and forces the old man to write a confession (the 'poem' I read to the audience at Harvard):

Ern Solomon Scat:

> *has failed*
> *fucks chooks*
> *fucks his family*
> *fucked all our family before him*

What is it that causes Ern's ultimate humiliation and the dignified triumph of Aboriginal people? For Kim Scott, it is a 'belief in a renewal of the flame of who and what has gone before'. It is an adherence to telling stories 'with a centre to which the alienated and marginalised might also belong'. And it is about having faith in the belief that out of 'ashes' comes 'renewal'.[14] Scott's writing not only addresses Noongar revitalisation – it creates it.

One more thing remains to be said about the larger frame for the novel's events. *Benang* has reinforced my understanding that Country and its guidance of human and non-human species has a major impact on the survival and cultural dynamism of Aboriginal people. As Uncle Jack reminds Harley towards the end of the novel, 'Those birds. That was the spirit of the land talking to you. Birds, animals, anything can do it. That is what Aboriginal people see.' Finally, Harley accepts the spirit of the land, along with the strength it provides Aboriginal people:

> Even now we gather, on chilly evenings, sometimes only a very few of us, sometimes more. We gather our strength in this way. From the heart all of us. Pale, burnt and shrivelled, I hover in the campfire smoke and sing as best I can. I am not alone ... we are still here, Benang.

THAT DEADMAN DANCE

Kim Scott published his next novel, *That Deadman Dance,* in 2010. The book has been discussed as a 'reconciliation novel', albeit one in which the concept fails. The description doesn't quite fit. The idea of linking reconciliation to first contact with Europeans is a little too 'cart before the horse'. It is not pedantic to argue that attempts at reconciliation between Aboriginal and Settler Australians were only possible *after* initial periods of invasion that saw frontier violence, land theft and stolen children. If Kim Scott has written a reconciliation novel, or at least one that deals with the traumas it involves, *Taboo*, published in 2017, is that novel, as it exposes the crimes of Settler violence, the impacts of lateral violence within Aboriginal

communities and the deep pain that true reconciliation will inevitably produce.

Natalie Quinlivan is correct to describe *That
Deadman Dance* as a novel ultimately concerned
with colonial paranoia and oppression, following
'the initial optimism of First Contact in King
George Sound', on the southern coast of Western Australia in the early nineteenth century.[15]
The optimism didn't last long at all. Early in
the novel, Menak, a Noongar leader, is already
suspicious of the motives of the recent white
arrivals on his Country:

> The ship settled, its sails furled. Menak
> had seen ships come and go since he was
> a child, had seen his father dance with the
> very earliest visitors. Not that he really
> remembered the incident, more the dance
> and song that lived on. It worried him that

these visitors didn't live up to the old stories, yet they stayed so long.

That Deadman Dance is a story of the failure of recognition on the part of this small group of British (mis)adventurers and opportunists. The Noongar people, on whose land the British (and American whalers) have arrived, do all they can to accommodate the visitors, through language, performance, mimicry and hospitality. These interactions with white people, from a Noongar perspective, are more than ceremonial. They guide white men through Country. In good faith, perhaps naïvely, considering what will occur, the visitors are shown where and how Country replenishes Noongar people:

In the course of the day their path (and inevitably, as they approached, Wooral's singing) led them to springs and water-holes, often concealed under overhanging rock, covered with slab, or in one case filled with pebbles.

A Noongar man, Bobby Wabalanginy, is a central character in the novel, from the moment of his birth into old age. He is witness to great change, from the early exchanges that suggest mutual accommodation to the eventual dispersal of Noongar people from their own Country, with Bobby reduced to the role of entertainer. Even so, he remains a powerful force in the story. As Bobby grows into adulthood and spends more time among white people, they treat him with affection, albeit that reserved for a curiosity and mascot. Yet he is far more than a harmless remnant, tolerated by colonial society for as long as he can perform and be laughed at.

The white family closest to Bobby, the Chaines, want to uplift Bobby, just as Ern Scat attempts to uplift Harley well over a century later (though without Ern's violence). He is tutored by Mrs Chaine. Her husband, who has requested that she provide guidance to Bobby, has clear intentions in mind: 'It is our moral duty to do so, her husband suggested, to help him move toward civilisation, and our friend Dr Cross has established it as a priority, to help save him.'

Bobby's own dilemma is whether to choose to be 'saved', and accept civilisation, or refuse the offer. It is a point of tension in the novel that also becomes a commentary on the wider forces informing the interactions between Noongar people and the new arrivals. A pair of Noongar runaways, 'outlaws' in the western sense, James and Jeffrey, cajole Bobby, tease him over his predicament. They want him to join them on their escapade. 'Come with us, Bobby,' they say. 'Leave these bloody white men.' They belittle him when he refuses their invitation: 'Bobby. You think you're a white boy now.'

Towards the end of the novel, Bobby continues to extend a hand of generosity to the visitors, who are now invaders of Country. 'This is my land, given to me by *Kongk* Menak,' Bobby sings. 'We will share it with you, and share what you bring,' he comments, as if the act of reciprocity were still possible. But the invaders are interested only in conquest and wish to share nothing. Bobby Wabalanginy could be read as a tragic figure, even a failure. If so, it is due to his sense of humanity, his belief in the common value of all people. He is unable to grasp the extent to which the arrival of strangers on Noongar Country is an inherently destructive act.

While Bobby may appear naïve to the threat posed by the strangers, some in the British party are under no illusion about the damage they have caused: 'A lot of his people had died, Mrs Chaine was coming to realise. Our arrival means their death, though we do not lift a hand.' Eventually, Bobby's performance, a welcoming song for the outsiders, is overwhelmed by gunshots and the aftermath of violence.

Scott writes a visceral scene into *That Deadman Dance*, one that stands for the wilful ignorance of those unable to imagine either a past governed by violence or a future based on recompense and reciprocity. Two male characters in the novel – one Noongar, the other British – are the central figures representing genuine attempts at accommodation and respect, followed by a failure of recognition, despite personal efforts to value each other as equals. Wunyeran is a respected Noongar leader. Dr Cross, a member of the British arrival party, values the original owners of Country and attempts to live on Country on Noongar terms. In a ceremonial and telling moment early in the story, Wunyeran persuades Cross to exchange his dress jacket for the cloak of another Noongar leader, Menak:

> The surprisingly soft and pliable kangaroo skin hung easily from Cross's shoulders, enclosing him in the smell of another man, a very different man, of course, but a man for all that. *Noongar*, he remembered.

Wunyeran and Dr Cross become such close friends that after their deaths they are initially buried in the same grave. This act of communion cannot be tolerated once it is made clear that Noongar Country is destined to become a permanent

British colony. The past, as immediate as it is, must be rewritten. The common grave is dug up and Wunyeran's remains are desecrated; 'The gravedigger's spade, working its way around Cross's coffin, broke and chipped Wunyeran's bones, exposed and disordered the skeleton.' The doctor's remains are also dug up and reinterred in the coloniser's King George cemetery. The act of violation is intended to ensure that Wunyeran and his community will be forgotten, so that the brief period of his white friend's life on Noongar Country can become a monument to empire:

Dr Joseph Cross

1781–1833

Surgeon Pioneer and Land Owner

1826–1833

King George Town Western Australia

TABOO AND RECOVERY

I n 2017, the Aboriginal author Melissa Lucashenko, who would also win the Miles Franklin (for her 2018 novel, *Too Much Lip*), wrote a review of Kim Scott's *Taboo*, a novel published seven years after *That Deadman Dance*. For Lucashenko, *Taboo* asks perhaps the most profound question of a nation grappling with the history of colonial violence and its contemporary manifestations, including endemic disadvantage and the continuation of lies and amnesia that refuse all attempts to heal, reconcile and act with responsibility. The existential question at the heart of *Taboo*, for Lucashenko, is: '[A]fter so much pain, after a history that has left so many of us incarcerated and broken, how can we possibly find peace together?'[16]

Taboo is set in present-day Western Australia, although, as with Scott's previous novels, it reaches back through colonial and contact history to the deep time of pre-invasion Noongar life. It is also grounded in a 'brutal modern reality' that Lucashenko attributes to the knowledge Scott gained when working with prisoners involved in the Wirlomin Noongar Language and Stories Project. A central character in the novel, Tilly, is a teenage Aboriginal girl. She has a white mother and a Noongar father, both of whom are deceased, resulting in Tilly searching for her extended Aboriginal family and community. Tilly suffers from self-harm. She has also been violently abused. And being biologically, if not culturally, simultaneously black and white, she represents a rift in Australian society that remains difficult to heal.

The 'taboo' of the story, in a direct sense,

relates to the fears of the Noongar community about visiting the location of a massacre that occurred on their Country. It is a sorry place, a site of taboo. An initiative of the white descendants of those responsible for the historical violence is met, unsurprisingly, with suspicion by the family and community members of those who were murdered. The stories contained in *Taboo* are more than symbolic of the challenges Australia faces in the twenty-first century. White Australia is a nation built on land theft and violence. All attempts to forget this history, either through pain or inconvenience, have failed. Regardless of the number of monuments erected to heroes, the creation of national myths of peaceful settlement and all attempts to exterminate Aboriginal identity, the truth returns again and again to undermine falsehoods. Tilly herself is a confronting presence. Her identity as a young Indigenous woman and the secrecy that surrounds her become the *real* problems for a colonial narrative dependent on amnesia for its power. Tilly is the secret who will not be silenced. It is not surprising, then, that the bodies of Aboriginal people have been made to disappear, by both physical and bureaucratic violence.

*

Across all his work, Kim Scott is concerned with the ethics of fiction and truth-telling. There is nothing contradictory in working with fiction rather than choosing the 'facts' of history, as there are few facts that can be relied upon when it comes to interrogating white Australia's myths of its colonial past. Nor are we well served by creating a simplistic ledger weighing the 'good' of the past against the 'bad'. If we are to shift the nation's psyche for the better, we must embrace stories of our colonial past, rather than bury them. And if we are to overcome discriminations embedded in contemporary Australia, we will need to tell *new stories*. This is the work that Kim Scott has been doing for many years, and we are in his debt. We would do well to accept the stories Scott has offered us with the same degree of generosity that he has shown towards his readers. Through his fiction, we are able to consider this country's past in a mature and ethical manner. He has laid the groundwork for other storytellers, be they a new generation of Indigenous writers or of Settler writers, including more recent immigrant and refugee writers who themselves wish to find new ways of telling.

I believe Kim Scott regards storytelling as an act of sharing, a communal venture, not unlike his involvement in the Wirlomin Noongar

Language and Stories Project. Here, Scott's is just one of many voices led by Elders. The goals of the project are to 'work to reclaim Wirlomin stories and dialect, in support of the maintenance of Noongar language, and to share them with Noongar families and communities as part of a process to claim, control and enhance Wirlomin Noongar cultural heritage'.

The Noongar community work on Country, gathering stories of people and place. One of the vibrant aspects of the venture is that Noongar stories are not a form of answering back – narratives produced to displace dominant stories of national triumphalism, or the myths of *Settlers toiling in a harsh and empty land*. Rather, Noongar stories are autonomous and independent, and precede the myths that were created to displace them. Listening to the recording of people speaking about the story project leaves the listener with a clear sense of what the oft-stated claim 'Always was, always will be' stands for in relation to everyday living, to life itself.

The Noongar nation hold stories reaching back tens of thousands of years, equipping them with the knowledge required to work with, and be with, Country. The power of their stories is remarkable, considering the devastation wrought on the community. Our understanding of their strength deepens with each story we hear or read. The project also records songs, shared on the Wirlomin website. Listening to them, I was reminded of both Harley in *Benang* and Bobby in *That Deadman Dance*. Both characters like to sing, and they understand the strategies of entertainment, which is yet another survival skill used to disarm Settlers who might otherwise do them harm.

The songs created by the project are entertaining, but they are so much more. They are 'contemporary Noongar interpretations of significant old songs from the south coast region of Western Australia between Esperance and Bremer Bay', and, along with the stories being documented, they 'reinforce bonds between individuals, community and place'. A third aspect of the project, linking both the songs and the storytelling, is an ever-growing word list. The Noongar dictionary revives the sounds, shapes and meaning of words, and this documentation and expression of the power of language is returned to often by Scott in his fiction.

When considering the writing of Kim Scott and the Wirlomin Noongar Language and Stories Project together, my own response is a deeply emotional one. I think of the terrible harm done to the Noongar men, women and children of *Benang*. All that these people wanted was the basic human right to *be*. They wanted to be with family and share a life on Country. And yet they were repeatedly violated. Murdered. Raped. Imprisoned. Their identities, as Aboriginal people, became the playthings of white men, sadistic men. In *That Deadman Dance*, Noongar welcomed the outsiders, who through greed and selfishness would eventually resort to theft and violence. *Taboo* epitomises both the sadness and strength of contemporary Noongar life: people never giving up, confronting adversity with the richness and depth of their culture.

Harley may occasionally appear lost, even bereft, in *Benang*. But he refuses to give up, or to give in to the notion that he may yet become 'the first white man born', and therefore lose connection with his true self and others. His eventual triumph is bound together with story: his uncles' stories, the stories of women relayed through the old men and, of course, Harley's own story. One of Bobby's skills in *That Deadman Dance* is that he not only entertains through storytelling but also ranges over time and place to gather vital stories of Noongar life, becoming the eye and ear of a history that might otherwise not be told. Both characters are a little restless, a required trait in one doing the work of collecting and gathering words, both foreign and familiar.

It may be presumptuous to say so, but after reading Kim Scott's novels and essays, and having come to know him personally, I suspect he has experienced periods of uncertainty and restlessness in his own life. We should not be surprised. After all, the colonial project has been centrally concerned with a desire to displace, to create a sense of uncertainty about who we are, to render Aboriginal people 'aliens in our own land'. Historically, white Australia was determined to own our identities, place them in a locked cupboard and deny us access to our very selves. Who wouldn't be restless, and perhaps uncertain, when faced with such psychological violence? Kim Scott, not unlike the characters in his novels, and alongside his family and community, has weathered a ferocious storm in his life. We are fortunate that he has survived to tell many tales. When I think of Kim, I smile gently, knowing that he has found his way home.

NOTES

1   Kim Scott, 'Covered up with sand', *Meanjin*,
    Winter 2007.

2   Warwick Anderson, *The Cultivation of Whiteness:
    Science, Health and Racial Destiny in Australia*,
    Melbourne University Press, Melbourne, 2003.

3   Ruby Lowe, 'Sexual and textual perversity
    in *Benang*' in *Kim Scott: Readers, Language,
    Interpretation*, edited by Philip Morrissey, Ruby
    Lowe and Marion Campbell, UWA Publishing,
    Crawley, 2019, pp. 23–36, p. 24.

4   Lisa Slater, 'Kim Scott's *Benang*: An ethics
    of uncertainty', research paper, University of
    Wollongong, 2005, pp. 147–58, p. 150.

5   For my essay on Alexis Wright see Tony Birch,
    'Sovereignty of imagination', *The Monthly*,
    April 2023, pp. 56–60.

6   Xavier Pons, '"I have to work through this
    white way of thinking": The deconstruction of
    discourses of whiteness in Kim Scott's *Benang*',
    Commonwealth Essays and Studies, vol. 30, no. 1,
    2007, pp. 37–48, p. 38.

7   Kim Scott, 'Racism burns Australia like a pox
        in a plague. We're not all in this together',
        The Guardian, 19 August 2020.

8   Summary of Justice Maurice O'Loughlin's
        judgement, published in *The Age*, 12 August 2000.

9   Scott, 'Covered up with sand'.

10   A.O. Neville, *Australia's Coloured Minority: Its Place
        in the Community*, Currawong Publishing Co.,
        Sydney, 1947, facing p. 57; facing p. 72.

11   Commonwealth of Australia, *Aboriginal Welfare:
        Initial Conference of Commonwealth and State
        Aboriginal Authorities*, Government Printer,
        Canberra, 21–23 April 1937, pp. 1–35, p. 2.

12   *Twenty-Third Report of the Board for the Protection of
        the Aborigines in the Colony of Victoria*, Government
        Printer, Melbourne, 1887, p. 4.

13   Neville, *Australia's Coloured Minority*, p. 122.

14   Kim Scott, 'Both hands full', *Westerly*, vol. 61, no. 1,
        2016, pp. 166–77.

15   Natalie Quinlivan, 'Finding a place in story: Kim
        Scott's writing and the Wirlomin Noongar Language
        and Stories Project', *Journal of the Association for the
        Study of Australian Literature*, , vol. 14, no. 3, 2014,
        pp. 1–12, p. 4.

16   Melissa Lucashenko, '*Taboo*: A masterful novel on the
        frontier of truth-telling', *The Guardian*, 25 July 2017.

BOOKS BY
KIM SCOTT

FICTION

True Country (1993)

Benang: From the Heart (1999)

Lost (2006)

That Deadman Dance (2010)

Taboo (2017)

NON-FICTION

Kayang and Me (with Hazel Brown, 2005)